So What's Wrong With Playing Video Games?

Written by
Joy Wilt Berry

Pictures by
Bartholomew

Educational Products Division

Producer Ron Berry
Editor Orly Kelly
Designer Abigail Johnston

No matter who you are or where you live, chances are you play video games. If this is true, you are like many other people. Recent surveys show that more time is spent playing video games than playing anything else.

Can playing video games hurt you?

Some parents, doctors, teachers and other concerned adults think that it can.

70467

Sometimes video games can provide an **escape from problems.** The games make it possible for people to run away from the things that are bothering them. Some people spend their time playing the games so that they will not have to face their problems.

Video games can also provide an **escape from responsibility**. The games encourage people to avoid doing the things they are supposed to do. Some people spend their time playing the games so that they will not have to work or do the things they do not want to do.

Too often video games can **take the place of friends and other people.** Some people choose to play video games over doing things with others. Unfortunately, they miss out on the wonderful experiences that are shared when people spend time together.

9

Video games can also **take the place of doing creative things.** People who spend all their free time playing the games may not have time to do other unique and exciting things. Thus, they themselves may become dull and boring.

Video games may cause a person to **become dependent**. People who spend all their free time playing the games may begin to depend on the games for entertainment. They may not deal with their boredom in creative, productive ways and might become very unhappy when there are no video games to occupy their time.

13

A person may **be dishonest** because of the video games. This can happen when the people who have become dependent on video games feel a need to play the games even when it is not best for them to do so. These people may lie to themselves or others in order to play the games.

A person may **spend too much money** on video games. This is because the games often have a hypnotic effect on people. Video games can cause them to play without realizing or caring how much money they are spending. These people are compelled to put money into the machines even when they should not be doing so. If they run out of money, they may steal so that they can continue to play the games.

Video games may cause a person to **become violent and perhaps even destructive.** This is because many of the video games subtly teach people that violence and destruction can lead to winning. They establish the winner as the one who destroys the most. Thus, destruction is shown to be an acceptable way to solve problems.

Obviously this is not good. Violence and destruction never solve anything. They only complicate situations and make things worse. Anything that encourages people to be violent or destructive is not good.

If it is true that video games may...

- provide an escape from problems,
- provide an escape from responsibility,
- take the place of friends and other people,
- take the place of doing creative things,
- cause a person to become dependent,
- cause a person to become dishonest,
- cause a person to spend too much money,
- cause a person to become aggressive and perhaps even violent,

...should anyone ever play video games? Should video games be banned? Should children be made to give them up?

Before you decide what should be done with video games, stop and think!

A video game is only an electrical machine. It cannot think. It cannot turn itself on or off.

But you can think, and you can turn a video game on and off.

You do not have to be controlled by a video game. Instead, you can and should control it.

Video games cannot hurt you if you control them and use them wisely.

In fact, a video game that is used properly can be a great source of fun and entertainment. It can also develop your hand/eye coordination.

It is not the video game that is good or bad; *it is the way you use the video game* that makes it good or bad.

There are several things that you must consider if you want to use video games properly.

They are...

- the **time** you spend playing the games,
- the **money** you spend playing the games,
- your **attitude** toward the games, and
- the **priority** you give to playing the games.

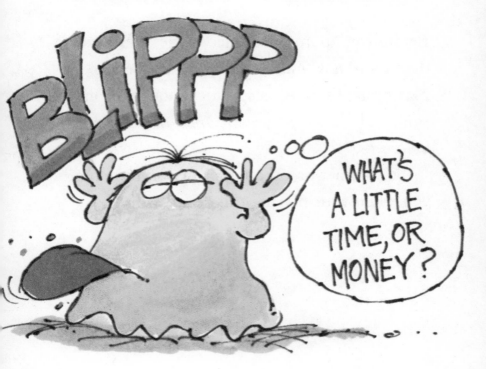

The Time You Spend Playing the Games

Before you approach a video game, you need to determine how much **time** you can spend playing it. Establish a specific amount of playing time and *do not play more than the allotted amount.*

Set a timer or ask another person to remind you when your playing time is up.

To help you decide upon a proper amount of playing time, you will need to determine how much **free time** you have.

Begin by thinking about a school day (or weekday). Consider the fact that there are 24 hours in a day. At least:

8 hours are spent sleeping,

1 hour is spent bathing, dressing and undressing,

3 hours are spent eating and with family, and

_8 hours are spent in and around school.

20 hours

If you subtract these 20 hours from the total of 24 hours, you get a remainder of 4 hours. You must now subtract the time it takes to do your work and take care of home responsibilities. What you have left will be the free time you have each day during the week.

Next, figure out how much free time you have on the weekend. Remember to consider the time that is spent. . .

- in church or temple,
- doing chores, and
- participating in family and group activities.

Once you know how much free time you have, you can determine how much time you can spend playing the games. Do this by listing all of the things you need or want to accomplish during your free time. Decide how much time these things will take. Remember to include...

- activities with clubs and organizations,
- lessons,
- sports,
- playing with friends,
- watching TV, and
- hobbies.

Any remaining free time can be spent playing video games.

With everything life has to offer, it is probable that you are spending too much time on video games if you are spending more than twenty-five percent of your free time playing them.

33

The Money You Spend Playing the Games

Before you approach a video game, you need to determine how much **money** you can spend playing it. Establish a specific amount of money and *do not spend more than the allotted amount.*

Do not go into a video game room carrying more money than you intend to spend. If you have an extra amount of money, ask a friend to hold it for you until you leave the video game room.

To help you decide how much money you can spend on video games, you will need to determine how much **extra spending money** you have.

Begin by listing your income. Your income is the money you expect to receive and includes your allowance and work earnings.

Next, list your expenses. Your expenses are the monies you plan to spend and should include your savings, donations, needs and wants.

You will know how much extra spending money you have when you subtract your expenses from your income.

With all of the worthwhile things there are to spend money on, you are probably spending too much money on video games if you spend more than twenty percent of your total income on them.

Your Attitude Toward the Games

The purpose of games is to bring fun and fulfillment or rest and relaxation into people's lives. Games that do not accomplish one or all of these things are pointless and should not be played.

If you experience fun and fulfillment or rest and relaxation when you play video games, you might want to continue to play them. If on the other hand you become frustrated, anxious or upset when you play the games, you should stop playing them.

Any game, including a video game, should make you feel good, not bad. It should bring you joy, not sadness.

39

The most important part of any game is how you feel or what you experience while you are playing it. This is more important than whether you win or lose, or get a high score.

When you play a game to win with no concern about what happens to you while you are playing, you are missing the point of the game. This is what is meant by the saying, "It's not whether you win or lose, but how you play the game that counts."

If you find when you play video games that winning, or beating your previous high score, becomes more important than playing, you should not play them.

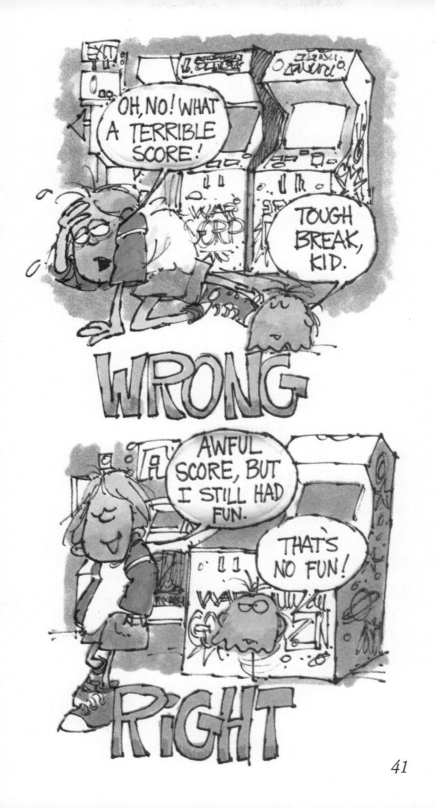

41

The Priority You Give to Playing the Games

The most important thing in your life is your survival and growth. Everything you do should contribute in one way or another to keeping you alive and to helping you become a healthy, productive person.

If video games keep you from doing the things that are good for you or if they hinder your growth in any way, you should not play them. In other words, you should stop playing the games if you spend so much time and energy playing them that you neglect your physical, mental or emotional health.

43

The second most important thing in your life is your relationship with other people. Doing things with others is important to your survival and growth.

If you are so busy playing video games that you are not spending time with other people, you should stop playing the games.

Thus, **you can make video games** a good or bad part of your life. It all depends on...

- how much time you spend playing the games,
- how much money you spend playing the games,
- your attitude toward the games, and
- the priority you give to playing the games.

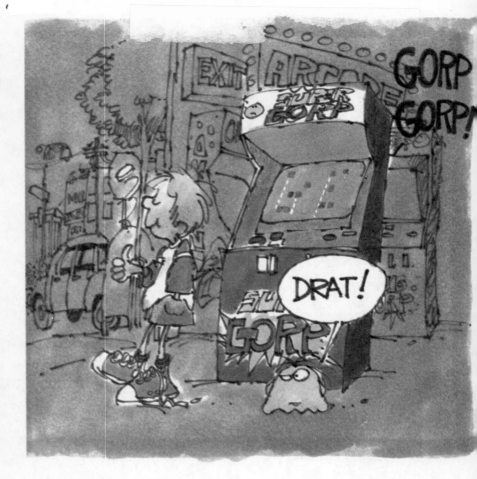

Just remember that how video games affect your
life is entirely dependent on how you use them.